London's Bendy B
2002 - 2011

A pictorial tribute
and fleet list

by

John Hypher

Published by Jacklyn Media

First Published 2012

ISBN 978-0-9571997-0-5

Published by Jacklyn Media
Suite 94 Dorset House
Duke Street
Chelmsford
CM1 1TB

Website: www.jacklynmedia.com
Email: enquiries@jacklynmedia.com

Layout and production by Lynda Hypher

Acknowledgements

All photographs are by the author unless otherwise credited.

Route leaflets, maps and posters are reproduced by kind permission of Transport for London. Thanks are also due to the PSV Circle and to the London Omnibus Traction Society (LOTS) for permission to reproduce vehicle information and to the credited photographers and bus companies for kindly allowing me to use their photographs. Thanks to Robin Lingwood for details of the Maltese registration numbers.

Also published by Jacklyn Media:

Carters Coaches (Ipswich)
25th Anniversary book

Cover photo:
London Central MAL74 on Westminster Bridge, November 2011

Rear cover photo:
London Central MAL75 picks up on Westminster Bridge September 2009

Title page photo:
Stagecoach East London 23034 passes the Tower of London during April 2011

Introduction

Bendy buses are a relatively recent phenomenon in the UK, having made their first appearance on these shores in the late 1970s and early 1980s. Although they had already been a familiar sight in Europe for several decades, they were not legalised here until 1980.

The first pioneering examples of both MAN and Leyland-DAB bendy buses were operated by South Yorkshire PTE with British Airways also running seven from the latter stable. The MAN vehicles were demonstrators and at least one of these later ran experimentally on the Oxford Park and Ride service. Whilst with NBC the author was fortunate enough to ride on several journeys between the car park and the city centre. These ran without problem and soon afterwards the author travelled on another bendy bus from Bristol to London and back for the Commercial Motor Show, happily without any problems being encountered.

The MANs were later operated for a short while by Midland Red West and Midland Red North. South Yorkshire PTE purchased further Leyland-DABs in 1985/6 and since then bendy buses have operated in small numbers in some of our UK towns and cities as well as on Park and Ride and Airport services.

In London the first bendy bus to be evaluated in service was one of the former South Yorkshire PTE vehicles, then operated by their successor, Mainline. This was C101 HDT, in Mainline's red and yellow livery but with the addition of Selkent and London Buses decals. It ran out of Plumstead Garage on service 180 between Abbey Wood and Catford Garage in April/May 1992. Also of note, sister vehicle C111 HDT was inspected by East London at Barking and West Ham during June 1991 but not operated in service.

Before bendy buses went into squadron service in London from 2002, First Centrewest undertook bendy bus trials with half a dozen Volvo/Wrightbus vehicles on the 207 Uxbridge Road service between October 2001 and April 2002. These buses were drafted in from First Hampshire and First Glasgow and run out of Greenford Garage between Shepherd Bush Green and Hayes by-Pass. They carried AV prefixes and ran in "Barbie" livery except for AV1 which was painted in London red.

London's first bendy bus routes were London General's Red Arrow services 507 and 521 which commenced operation on 5 June 2002 between Waterloo and Victoria/London Bridge respectively. Since then bendy buses have additionally both started and ceased operating on routes 12, 18, 25, 29, 38, 73, 149, 436 and 453 with the 207 being the last route to succumb on 9 December 2011. During that time more than 400 bendy buses were operated along the capital's streets by Arriva, First, Go-Ahead Group and Stagecoach.

London's bendy buses received notoriety during the latter part of 2003 and early 2004 when three of their number quite spectacularly caught fire and were destroyed whilst operating on route 436. As a result on-board measures were put into place to counteract such problems occurring in future, with a large degree of success, as no further bendies were totally destroyed.

Their withdrawal from service in London was political and was one of the platforms upon which Boris Johnson, the Mayor of London, was elected to office. This pledge has been fulfilled and the debate for and against bendy buses in London falls beyond the scope of this volume.

Photographs are arranged in route number order followed by a selection of images showing former London bendy buses in new liveries and performing new duties elsewhere from Park and Ride services in Bristol, to new overseas routes in Malta! At the rear of this book are tables listing all of London's bendy buses together with a table of services operated by these vehicles with dates of commencement and withdrawal. Happily some of the redundant bendies will re-emerge to make a brief appearance during the 2012 Olympics and a handful will be retained for private hire work for the time being.

Enjoy!

MAL65 at Peckham Road, June 2010

London Central

- Oxford Circus ⊖
- Piccadilly Circus ⊖
- Trafalgar Square ⊖ ⇌
- Westminster ⊖
- Elephant & Castle ⊖ ⇌
- Camberwell Green
- Peckham
- Dulwich

London Buses

Route 12
is getting better from every angle

From Saturday 6 November 2004 new bendy buses will be on route 12

24 hour service

Oxford Circus – Elephant & Castle – Dulwich

MAYOR OF LONDON   Transport for London

MAL65 in Whitehall, September 2009

MAL65 in Etherow Street, Dulwich, July 2010

MAL64 at Trafalgar Square, September 2010

MAL71 in Lordship Lane, Dulwich on the last day of operation on 4th November 2011

MAL84 at the Elephant and Castle, June 2010

MAL68 at Peckham Rye, a very gloomy last day of bendy buses on the 12 on 4th November 2011

MAL80 turns into Regent Street from its layover point in Cavendish Place, September 2010

MAL86 at The Elephant and Castle, the last day of route 12 bendy buses on 4th November 2011

- Euston Station ⊖ ⇌
- Euston Square ⊖
- University College Hospital
- Warren Street ⊖
- Great Portland Street ⊖
- Regent's Park Station ⊖
- Marylebone Road
- Baker Street Station ⊖
- Marylebone Station ⊖ ⇌
- Edgware Road ⊖
- Paddington Green
- Royal Oak Station ⊖
- Harrow Road
- Kensal Green ⊖ ⇌
- Harlesden
- Stonebridge Park ⊖ ⇌
- Wembley Central ⊖ ⇌
- Sudbury ⇌

London Buses

Route 18 is getting better from every angle

From Saturday 15 November 2003 new Bendy Buses will be on route 18

Euston – Marylebone – Sudbury

MAYOR OF LONDON   Transport for London

First

EA11012 at Euston Station, October 2009

Image on page 9: EA11022 in Harrow Road close to junction with Sutherland Avenue, June 2010

EA11014 in Harrow Road / Sutherland Avenue, June 2010

EA11055 pulls away from Euston Station, June 2010

EA11013 at Royal Oak, September 2010

EA11028 pauses at Sudbury before departure back to Euston, June 2010

EA11024 travels along the A404 close to Shakespeare Crescent, June 2010

EA11008 at Shakespeare Crescent on the A404, June 2010

EA11029 picks up at Sutherland Avenue / Harrow Road, June 2010

EA11011 in Harrow Road / Cirencester Street, September 2010

EA11039 at Sutherland Avenue bus stop in Harrow Road, June 2010

East London

23075 at Stepney Green Station, September 2010

London Buses

Route 25 is getting better from every angle

From Saturday 26 June 2004
new Bendy Buses will be on route 25

24 hour service

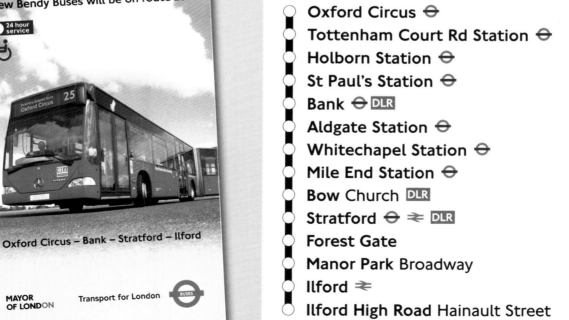

Oxford Circus – Bank – Stratford – Ilford

MAYOR OF LONDON   Transport for London

○ **Oxford Circus** ⊖
○ **Tottenham Court Rd Station** ⊖
○ **Holborn Station** ⊖
○ **St Paul's Station** ⊖
○ **Bank** ⊖ DLR
○ **Aldgate Station** ⊖
○ **Whitechapel Station** ⊖
○ **Mile End Station** ⊖
○ **Bow** Church DLR
○ **Stratford** ⊖ ≷ DLR
○ **Forest Gate**
○ **Manor Park** Broadway
○ **Ilford** ≷
○ **Ilford High Road** Hainault Street

23077 is pictured at Showbus, Duxford when just a few months old in September 2004

23034 is seen at West Ham Garage in University of East London overall advertisement livery, June 2008

23032 at Bank, April 2011

23045 at St Paul's, April 2011

23070 in New Change during September 2010

23042 at Stratford Bus Station, September 2010,

203054 in Ilford, September 2010

23027 at Tottenham Court Road Station, October 2009

19

23037 at Stratford, September 2010

23068 at Mile End Station, September 2010

Arriva

29

	Trafalgar Square for Charing Cross ⊖ ≥
7	**Tottenham Court Road Station** ⊖
5	**Warren Street Station** ⊖
9	**Camden Town** ⊖
8	**Holloway** Nag's Head
6	**Finsbury Park Station** ⊖ ≥
4	**Manor House** ⊖
10	**Turnpike Lane Station** ⊖
6	**Wood Green Station** ⊖

Off peak journey times between stops in minutes
Operated by **Arriva London**

Commencing 14th January 2006

MA156 at Wood Green, July 2010

MA153 and MA125 inside Wood Green Depot, July 2010

MA149 at Trafalgar Square, September 2010

MA135 at Trafalgar Square, July 2010

An unidentified MA straddles Whitehall, on the last day of service, 25 November 2011

MA137 at Manor House, September 2010

MA154 at Cambridge Circus, October 2009

MA151 at Warren Street, September 2010

MA149 at Finsbury Park, September 2010

Arriva

Clapton Pond Terminus, September 2009

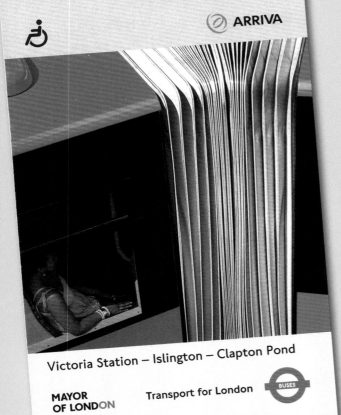

London Buses

Route 38
is changing from every angle
From Saturday 29 October 2005
new bendy buses will be on route 38

♿ ⊘ ARRIVA

Victoria Station – Islington – Clapton Pond

MAYOR
OF LONDON   Transport for London   BUSES

- Victoria Station ⊖ ≷
- Hyde Park Corner ⊖
- Green Park Station ⊖
- Piccadilly Circus ⊖
- Tottenham Court Road Station ⊖
- Holborn Station ⊖ (westbound only)
- Holborn (Theobald's Road)
- Rosebery Avenue
- Islington Angel ⊖
- Essex Road
- Dalston Junction
- Hackney Central Station ≷
- Clapton Pond

MA123 at the Trocadero, October 2009

MA79 at Hackney, October 2009

MA98 in a special livery for 'China in London' at Old Park Lane, April 2006 **Photo:** Dave Heath

MA125 at Victoria Bus Station, September 2009

MA110 in Essex Road, Islington, September 2009

MA105 in Essex Road Islington at dusk, September 2009

MA100 in Graham Road, September 2009

MA112 crosses Cambridge Circus, October 2009

MA103 in Hackney, October 2009

MA120 at Tottenham Court Road Station, October 2009

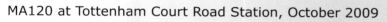

Arriva

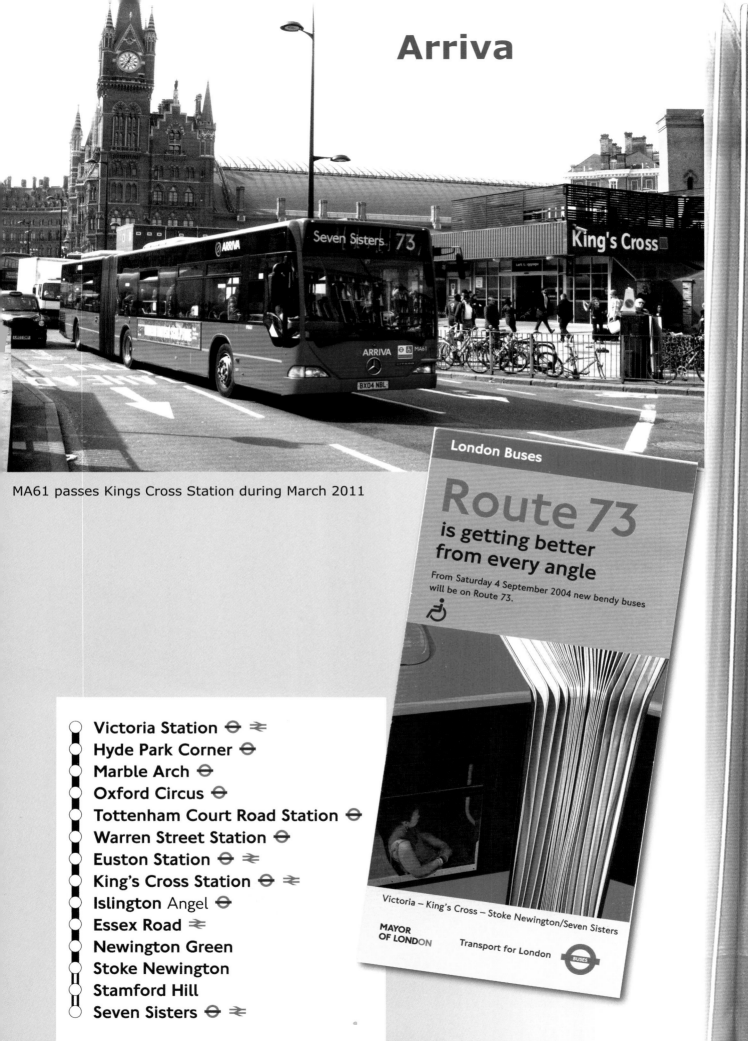

MA61 passes Kings Cross Station during March 2011

London Buses

Route 73
is getting better from every angle

From Saturday 4 September 2004 new bendy buses will be on Route 73.

Victoria – King's Cross – Stoke Newington/Seven Sisters

MAYOR OF LONDON   Transport for London

- Victoria Station ⊖ ≷
- Hyde Park Corner ⊖
- Marble Arch ⊖
- Oxford Circus ⊖
- Tottenham Court Road Station ⊖
- Warren Street Station ⊖
- Euston Station ⊖ ≷
- King's Cross Station ⊖ ≷
- Islington Angel ⊖
- Essex Road ≷
- Newington Green
- Stoke Newington
- Stamford Hill
- Seven Sisters ⊖ ≷

MA87 at Stamford Hill in April 2011

MA60 emerges from White Lion Street, Islington in March 2011

MA65 joins Euston Road from Churchway in June 2010

MA58 leaves Euston Station during September 2010

MA57 at Marble Arch during October 2011

MA89 at Stoke Newington Common in April 2011

MA70 at Church Walk, Stoke Newington in September 2011

MA52 at Clissold Crescent, Stoke Newington during September 2011

MA16 lays over at Victoria Bus Station, November 2009

Images on pages 38 and 39: interior views of Arriva MA 83 and cab view of MA80

MA52 drops off in Buckingham Palace Road, Victoria in September 2011

1 Pay before you board

Cash is not accepted on the new Bendy Buses. So you must have a ticket **before** you board. There are two ways you can pay before you board:

Roadside ticket machines

- These can be found at every stop along the route and sell Adult and Child single tickets as well as One Day Bus Passes

- You need the exact money as the machines do not give change

- The machines take the following coins £2, £1, 50p, 20p, 10p and 5p

Ticket outlets

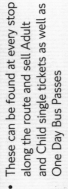

- Travelcards, Bus Passes and Savers can be bought wherever you see the new Ticket Stop sign

- London Underground stations sell Travelcards, Bus Passes and Savers

- National Rail stations sell Travelcards

2 Three door entry

Passengers with a Travelcard, Bus Pass, freedom pass or a single journey ticket can board through any of the three doors.

Saver tickets: Saver ticket holders must board through the front door and present their ticket to the driver as usual.

Easier access: Wheelchair users should get on through the low-floor central door which is fitted with a ramp.

3 Fully accessible

Bendy Buses are fitted with climate control and enhanced security with CCTV. The buses are low floor which means they are accessible for everyone.

MA9 crosses London Bridge in September 2009

London Buses

Route 149 is changing from every angle

From Saturday 24 April 2004 new Bendy Buses will be on route 149

24 hour service

London Bridge – Stamford Hill – Edmonton Green

MAYOR OF LONDON   Transport for London   BUSES

London Bridge Station
Monument Station
Liverpool Street Station
Shoreditch Church
Kingsland Road
Dalston Junction
Stoke Newington
Stamford Hill Broadway
Seven Sisters Station
Bruce Grove
White Hart Lane
Upper Edmonton Angel Corner
Edmonton Green Station

MA75 pulls away from London Bridge Station in September 2010

MA59 is seen in Shoreditch High Street in September 2010

MA69 lays over at Edmonton Green Bus Station in October 2009

MA10 approaches Liverpool Street Station during October 2009

MA46 at London Bridge Station in September 2010

MA46 in Shoreditch High Street during September 2010

MA58 in Bishopsgate during September 2009

MA60 picks up at London Bridge during September 2009

EA11053 at Ealing during October 2011

London Buses

Route 207

is changing from every angle

From Saturday 9 April 2005 new bendy buses will be on a revised route 207.

First transforming travel

Shepherd's Bush Green – Ealing – Hayes By-pass

MAYOR OF LONDON   Transport for London   BUSES

- **Shepherd's Bush Green** ⊖
- **Acton Vale**
- **Acton** Old Town Hall
- **Acton High St** King St
- **Ealing Common** ⊖
- **Ealing Broadway** ⊖ ≥
- **West Ealing** Broadway
- **Hanwell** Broadway
- **Ealing Hospital** Uxbridge Rd
- **Southall Broadway**
- **Hayes** By-pass

Route 207 was extended from Shepherds Bush Green to the new White City Bus Station in November 2008

First

EA11052 at Hayes By-Pass on 9th December 2011

EA11000, formerly a demonstrator, at Hanger Lane on the last day of operation, 9th December 2011

EA11051 approaches Shepherds Bush Station on 9th December 2011

EA11005 at Ealing Hospital in September 2010

EA11046 at White City during November 2011

EA11041 at Acton Central on 9th December 2011

EA11042 lays over at White City Bus Station during September 2010

EA11045 at Loftus Road during September 2010

EA11061 at Ealing during October 2011

EA11049 at The Lido, West Ealing on the last day of operation, 9th December 2011

MAL57 at the Lewisham Centre Terminus on the last day of operation 18 November 2011

NEW BUS ROUTE
436

New bus route from 8 February 2003

Paddington
Victoria
Lewisham

New route 436

Paddington Station ⊖ ≷

Marble Arch ⊖

Hyde Park Corner ⊖

Victoria Station ⊖ ≷

Vauxhall Station ⊖ ≷

Oval Station ⊖

Camberwell Green

Peckham

New Cross Gate ⊖ ≷

Lewisham Station ≷ DLR

Lewisham *Lewisham Centre*

MAL41 at Victoria Station during September 2009

MAL51 approaches Vauxhall Bus Station in October 2010

MAL38 lays over at Paddington during August 2008

MAL55 at Victoria Bus Station during September 2009

MAL37 at New Cross Gate Station in July 2010

MAL45 approaches Victoria Bus Station during September 2011

MAL32 adjacent to the rail station in Lewisham on the last day of operation 18 November 2011

MAL53 makes a sharp left hand turn as it leaves Vauxhall Bus Station on 18 November 2011

MORE BUS, LESS FUSS

453

New bendy buses on route 453/N453 from 15 March 2003

Marylebone
Oxford Circus
Deptford

24 hour service

Route 453/N453

MAYOR OF LONDON

Buses are getting better

BUSES

Brand New 23016 was photographed in Whithall during the spring 2003. **Photo:** Author's collection

Selkent
until 15th February 2008

Marylebone Station ⊖ ⇌
Baker Street Station ⊖
Regent's Park ⊖
Oxford Circus ⊖
Piccadilly Circus ⊖
Trafalgar Square ⊖ ⇌
Westminster ⊖ ⛴
Elephant & Castle ⊖ ⇌
Old Kent Road
New Cross Gate ⊖ ⇌
Deptford Broadway

London General
from 16th February 2008

Selkant 23021 at Trafalgar Square during April 2007 **Photo:** MS Doggett

23013 shows off its Stagecoach livery to advantage as it makes it way towards Marylebone Station. **Photo:** author's collection

MAL115 at New Cross Bus Garage on a short working during September 2011

MAL102 in Regent Street during September 2010

MAL116 in New Kent Road, close to the Elephant and Castle during April 2011

MAL112 lays over at Marylebone Station in September 2010

MAL110 on Westminster Bridge during June 2010

MAL96 passes along Whitehall during September 2011

MAL102 crosses Westminster Bridge during October 2010

MAL107 at the Deptford Bridge Terminus in September 2011

London General

521

- Waterloo Station ⊖ ⇌
- Waterloo Bridge
  South Bank Complex
- Lancaster Place * (to London Bridge)
  or St Mary-le-Strand (to Waterloo)
- Aldwych *
- Holborn Station ⊖
  Kingsway
- Holborn Proctor Street
  (stops in High Holborn to Waterloo)
- High Holborn
  Brownlow Street
- Holborn Circus
- City Thameslink Station ⇌
  Holborn Viaduct
- St Paul's Station ⊖
- Mansion House Station ⊖
- Cannon Street Station ⊖ ⇌
- London Bridge Station ⊖ ⇌

* Northbound buses will run via Kingsway Subway during the morning and evening peaks and via Aldwych during the day.

Southbound buses will always run via Aldwych.

Red Arrow routes 507 & 521

Changes from 5 June 2002

More bus, less fuss

Buses are getting better

MAYOR OF LONDON

507

- Waterloo Station ⊖ ⇌
- Shell Centre (to Victoria only)
- St Thomas' Hospital
- Lambeth Bridge
- Horseferry Road
  Millbank
- Horseferry Road
  Marsham Street
- Horseferry Road
  Strutton Ground
- Victoria Street
  Army & Navy
- Westminster Cathedral
- Victoria Station ⊖ ⇌

MAL10 at Victoria Bus Station **Photo:** Author's collection

MAL3 crosses Waterloo Bridge during October 2008 **Photo:** MS Doggett

MAL28 at London Bridge in June 2007 **Photo:** MS Doggett

MAL13 at Victoria in July 2002, just a month after the start of Bendybus operation in London
Photo: Alan Conway

MAL28 at Waterloo in June 2003 **Photo:** Tony Cutler

MAL1 at London Bridge, June 2007 **Photo:** MS Doggett

Rail Replacement Services

MA83 passes Royal Victoria Station en-route to the Excel Centre while on rail replacement stand-by duties on 10th November 2011

MA81 and other buses in the MA80 series on stand-by duties at the Excel Centre on 10th November 2011. This was the last duty that Arriva London bendy buses carried out before final withdrawal from London.

London General MAL15 loads passengers and Redhill Station on rail replacement duties to Gatwick Airport and Three Bridges on 28th December 2006 **Photo:** Alan Conway

Although not rail replacement as such, London General MAL6 runs from Epsom Station on Epsom race day special route 406F on Derby Day, 6th June 2009 **Photo:** Dave Heath

Pastures New

Brighton & Hove 103 at North Weald Bus Rally July 2010. This was formerly London General Red Arrow MAL10. Note the removal of the centre doors for use on University service 25 in Brighton

Wilts & Dorset 4001 was previously London General Red Arrow MAL15 and is seen at their Swanage Depot in August 2010. Its normal route is the U1 Bournemouth University service.

Go-NorthEast 5346 was previously MAL117 in the London General fleet. It is now used on City Link route 58. **Photo:** courtesy of Go-NorthEast

Former Arriva MA164 (previously Selkent 23012) is one of several former London Bendy buses in use on car park duties at Stansted Airport. It is seen laying over in February 2011.

CT Plus MCA14 was previously London General Red Arrow MAL5. It is now used on the Brislington Park & Ride service 904 in Bristol and was photographed in September 2011 leaving Brislington car park.

Formerly London General Red Arrow MAL2, CT Plus MCA13 approaches Brislington car park during September 2011 while on Park & Ride duties in Bristol.

A number of former Selkent bendy buses have been used on internal staff transport at the Olympic site in Stratford by CT Plus. Dwarfed by the Olympic stadium is MCA2 (previously Selkent 23020) in October 2010.

Konectbus 803 is pictured at Costessey car park, Norwich in January 2012 on Park & Ride route 604. This bus was previously MAL110 in the London General Fleet

A large number of Arriva London bendy buses have been shipped to Malta for service there following Arriva winning the contract to provide services on the Island. As yet unregistered, one of these former London Buses poses at Malta Airport prior to entering service. **Photo:** Courtesy of Arriva

Still in London red complete with MAL96 fleet numbers, Konect Bus pressed this vehicle into service prior to repaint on the Costessey Park & Ride service 604. It was photographed at Costessey car park in January 2012. This bus was previously in the London General fleet.

Arriva Merseyside 6014 was numbered MA14 while in London and was photographed on the 501 Air Link service at John Lennon Airport, Liverpool. This is one of a pair of these buses painted in this special blue livery. Note the removal of the centre doors. **Photo:** Author's collection.

Arriva Midlands 5004 is now used on the 80 UNIlinx University service in Leicester. This bus was previously MA10 in the Arriva London fleet. **Photo:** Author's collection

Table 1 Bendybus Routes/Dates

Route No.	From	To	Operator	Introduced	Withdrawn	Previous Bus Type	Current Bus Type
12	Oxford Circus	Dulwich	London Central	6 Nov 2004	4 Nov 2011	Routemaster RML	Volvo B5LH /Gemini 2 'WHV' plus Volvo B9TL /Gemini 2 'WVL'
18	Euston	Sudbury	First London	15 Nov 2003	12 Nov 2010	Trident/Plaxton 'TN'	Volvo B9TL/ Gemini 2 'VN'
25	Oxford Circus	Ilford	Stagecoach East London	26 Jun 2004	24 Jun 2011	Trident/Plaxton/ Alexander 'TAL/TN/TNL' First London	Volvo B9TL/ Gemini 2 'VN' First London
29	Trafalgar Square	Wood Green	Arriva London North	14 Jan 2006	25 Nov 2011	DAF/Plaxton 'DLP'	Wrightbus Gemini 2 DL 'DW'
N29	Trafalgar Square	Enfield Town	Arriva London North	15 Jan 2006	25 Nov 2011	DAF/Plaxton 'DLP'	Wrightbus Gemini 2 DL 'DW'
38	Victoria	Clapton Pond	Arriva London North	29 Oct 2005	13 Nov 2009	Routemaster RML	AD Trident/ Enviro 400 'T' plus Wrightbus Gemini 2 DL 'DW'
73	Victoria	Stoke Newington/ Seven Sisters	Arriva London North	4 Sept 2004	2 Sept 2011	Routemaster RML	Volvo B5LH /Gemini 2 'HV' plus Wrightbus Gemini 2 DL 'DW'
149	London Bridge	Edmonton Green	Arriva London North	24 Apr 2004	15 Oct 2010	DAF/Alexander 'DLA'	Wrightbus Gemini 2 DL 'DW'
207	Shepherds Bush Green (later White City)	Hayes By-Pass	First London	9 Apr 2005	9 Dec 2011	Trident/Plaxton 'TNL'	Scania Omnicity 'SN'
436	Paddington	Lewisham	London Central	8 Feb 2003	18 Nov 2011	N/A	AD Trident/ Enviro 400/400H 'E/EH'
453/ N453	Marylebone	Deptford	Stagecoach Selkent	15 Mar 2003	15 Feb 2008 Contract Change	N/A	N/A
453/ N453	Marylebone	Deptford	London General	16 Feb 2008	23 Sep 2011	N/A	AD Trident/ Enviro 400 'E'
507	Waterloo	Victoria	London General	5 Jun 2002	24 Jul 2009	LN Greenway 'GLS'	Mercedes-Benz Citaro 'MEC'
521	Waterloo	London Bridge	London General	5 Jun 2002	28 Aug 2009	LN Greenway 'GLS'	Mercedes-Benz Citaro 'MEC'

London Bendybus Fleet List

All London Bendybuses were Mercedes-Benz Citaro 0530G models with Mercedes-Benz AB49T bodywork
All are 18 metres in length

Table 2 Stagecoach Selkent/East London

Fleet No.	Reg. No.	New	1st alloc.	Final alloc.	Withdrawn	Initial disposal (via Dawsonrentals)	Notes
23001	LV52 VFW	12/02	PD	PD	09/06	First Centrewest 11066	S
23002	LV52 VFX	02/03	PD	PD	09/06	First Centrewest 11067	S O/A
23003	LV52 VFY	02/03	PD	PD	09/06	First Centrewest 11068	S
23004	LV52 VFZ	02/03	PD	PD	09/06	First Centrewest 11069	S
23005	LV52 VGA	02/03	PD	PD	02/08	Arriva London North MA 161	S
23006	LX03 HCE	03/03	PD	PD	02/08	Arriva London North MA 162	S
23007	LX03 HCF	03/03	PD	PD	02/08	CT Plus, Hackney MCA 3	S
23008	LX03 HCG	03/03	PD	PD	02/08	Arriva London North MA 163	S
23009	LX03 HCH	03/03	PD	PD	02/08	CT Plus, Hackney MCA 7	S
23010	LX03 HCJ	03/03	PD	PD	02/08	CT Plus, Hackney MCA 5	S
23011	LX03 HCK	03/03	PD	PD	02/08	CT Plus, Hackney MCA 11	S
23012	LX03 HCL	03/03	PD	PD	02/08	Arriva London North MA 164	S
23013	LX03 HCN	03/03	PD	PD	02/08	CT Plus, Hackney MCA 10	S
23014	LX03 HCP	03/03	PD	PD	02/08	CT Plus, Hackney MCA 4	S
23015	LX03 HCU	03/03	PD	PD	02/08	Arriva London North MA 165	S
23016	LX03 HCV	03/03	PD	PD	02/08	CT Plus, Hackney MCA 12	S
23017	LX03 HCY	03/03	PD	PD	02/08	CT Plus, Hackney MCA 6	S
23018	LX03 HCZ	03/03	PD	PD	02/08	CT Plus, Hackney MCA 1	S
23019	LX03 HDC	03/03	PD	WH	02/08,06/11	East London 23019; Dawsonrentals	S
23020	LX03 HDD	03/03	PD	PD	02/08	CT Plus, Hackney MCA 2	S
23021	LX03 HDE	03/03	PD	PD	02/08	Arriva North London MA 166	S
23022	LX03 HDF	03/03	PD	PD	02/08	Dawsonrentals	S
23023	LX03 HDG	03/03	PD	PD	02/08	CT Plus, Hackney MCA 13	S
23024	LX03 HDH	03/03	PD	PD	02/08	First Centrewest 11084	S
23025	LX03 HDJ	03/03	PD	PD	02/08	CT Plus, Hackney MCA 8	S
23026	LX03 HDK	03/03	PD	PD	02/08	CT Plus, Hackney MCA 9	S
23027	LX03 HDL	03/03	PD	WH	02/08,06/11	East London 23027; Dawsonrentals	S
23028	LX03 HDN	03/03	PD	WH	02/08,06/11	East London 23028; Dawsonrentals	S
23029	LX03 HDU	03/03	PD	WH	02/08,06/11	East London 23029; Dawsonrentals	S
23030	LX03 HDV	03/03	PD	PD	02/08	London Central MAL 120	S
23031	LX03 HDY	03/03	PD	WH	06/11	To East London 23031; Dawsonrentals	S O/A
23032	LX03 HDZ	03/03	PD	WH	06/11	To East London 23032; Dawsonrentals	S
23033	LX03 HEJ	03/03	PD	WH	06/11	To East London 23033; Dawsonrentals	S O/A
23034	LX03 HEU	03/03	PD	WH	06/11	To East London 23034; Dawsonrentals	S O/A
23035	LX03 HEV	03/03	PD	WH	06/11	To East London 02/05; Dawsonrentals	S
23036	LX04 KZG	06/04	WA	WH	06/11	Dawsonrentals	E
23037	LX04 KZJ	06/04	WA	WH	06/11	Dawsonrentals	E

No.	Reg					Operator	Notes
23038	LX04 KZK	06/04	WA	WH	06/11	Dawsonrentals	E
23039	LX04 KZL	06/04	WA	WH	06/11	Dawsonrentals	E
23040	LX04 KZM	06/04	WA	WH	06/11	Dawsonrentals	E
23041	LX04 KZN	05/04	WA	WH	06/11	Dawsonrentals	E
23042	LX04 KZP	06/04	WA	WH	06/11	Dawsonrentals	E
23043	LX04 KZR	06/04	WA	WH	06/11	Dawsonrentals	E
23044	LX04 KZS	05/04	WA	WH	06/11	Dawsonrentals	E
23045	LX04 KZT	05/04	WA	WH	06/11	Dawsonrentals	E
23046	LX04 KZU	05/04	WA	WH	06/11	Dawsonrentals	E
23047	LX04 KZV	06/04	WA	WH	06/11	Dawsonrentals	E
23048	LX04 KZW	06/04	WA	WH	06/11	Dawsonrentals	E
23049	LX04 KZY	06/04	WA	WH	06/11	Dawsonrentals	E
23050	LX04 KZZ	06/04	WA	WH	06/11	Dawsonrentals	E
23051	LX04 LBA	06/04	WA	WH	06/11	Dawsonrentals	E
23052	LX04 LBE	06/04	WA	WH	06/11	Dawsonrentals	E
23053	LX04 LBF	06/04	WA	WH	06/11	Dawsonrentals	E
23054	LX04 LBG	06/04	WA	WH	06/11	Dawsonrentals	E
23055	LX04 LBJ	06/04	WA	WH	06/11	Dawsonrentals	E
23056	LX04 LBK	06/04	WA	WH	06/11	Dawsonrentals	E
23057	LX04 LBL	06/04	WA	WH	06/11	Dawsonrentals	E
23058	LX04 LBN	06/04	WA	WH	06/11	Dawsonrentals	E
23059	LX04 LBP	06/04	WA	WH	06/11	Dawsonrentals	E
23060	LX04 LBU	06/04	WA	WH	06/11	Dawsonrentals	E
23061	LX04 LBV	06/04	WA	WH	06/11	Dawsonrentals	E
23062	LX04 LBY	06/04	WA	WH	06/11	Dawsonrentals	E
23063	LX04 LBZ 630 DYE 8/06	06/04	WA	WH	06/11	Dawsonrentals	E, R
23064	LX04 LCA	06/04	WA	WH	06/11	Dawsonrentals	E
23065	LX04 LCC	06/04	WA	WH	06/11	Dawsonrentals	E
23066	LX04 LCE	06/04	WA	WH	06/11	Dawsonrentals	E
23067	LX04 LCF	06/04	WA	WH	06/11	Dawsonrentals	E
23068	LX04 LCG	06/04	WA	WH	06/11	Dawsonrentals	E
23069	LX04 LCJ	06/04	WA	WH	06/11	Dawsonrentals	E
23070	LX04 LCK	06/04	WA	WH	06/11	Dawsonrentals	E
23071	LX04 LCM	06/04	WA	WH	06/11	Dawsonrentals	E
23072	LX04 LCN	06/04	WA	WH	06/11	Dawsonrentals	E
23073	LX04 LCP	06/04	WA	WH	06/11	Dawsonrentals	E
23074	LX04 LCT	06/04	WA	WH	06/11	Dawsonrentals	E
23075	LX04 LCU	06/04	WA	WH	06/11	Dawsonrentals	E
23076	LX04 LCV WLT 886 10/04	06/04	WA	WH	06/11	Dawsonrentals	E, T
23077	LX04 LCW VLT 240 11/04	06/04	WA	WH	06/11	Dawsonrentals	E, R

Notes to Stagecoach Fleet List

23001 – 23030 withdrawn following loss of contract for service 453 to London General

23031 – 23077 withdrawn following conversion of service 25 to double deck and loss of contract to First Centrewest

Stagecoach London sold to Macquarie Bank June 2006 who operated as the East London Group. Stagecoach re-purchased the East London Group in October 2010.

Key to notes column:- S = Selkent   E = East London   O/A = Overall advertisement   R = regained original registration number 07/11   T= regained original registration number 11/07

Overall advertisements were carried by 23002 for Oyster Cards in 2004 with blue background; 23031 carried a multicoloured advert showing a parkland scene for an air quality campaign; 23033 carried 2 designs for the University of East London 2005-8 with blue backgrounds; 23034 for the University of East London 2005-8 with an orange background.

Depot Codes: PD = Plumstead   WA = Waterden Road   WH = West Ham

Waterden Road Closed in December 2007 with vehicles moving temporarily to Rainham (RM) until May 2008 when they went to West Ham

Table 3   First London {CentreWest London Buses Ltd}

Fleet No.	Reg. No.	New	1st alloc.	Final alloc.	Withdrawn	Initial disposal	Notes
EA 11000	BX54 EBC	09/06	WJ	HS	12/11	Store	D
EA 11001	LK53 FAA	10/03	WJ	WJ	11/10	Dawsonrentals	
EA 11002	LK53 FAF	10/03	WJ	WJ	11/10	Dawsonrentals	
EA 11003	LK53 FAJ	11/03	WJ	WJ	11/10	Dawsonrentals	
EA 11004	LK53 FAM	11/03	WJ	WJ	11/10	Dawsonrentals	
EA 11005	LK53 FAO	11/03	WJ	HS	06/11	Dawsonrentals	
EA 11006	LK53 FAU	11/03	WJ	WJ	11/10	Dawsonrentals	
EA 11007	LK53 FBA	10/03	WJ	WJ	11/10	Dawsonrentals	
EA 11008	LK53 FBB	11/03	WJ	WJ	11/10	Dawsonrentals	
EA 11009	LK53 FBC	10/03	WJ	HS	06/11	Dawsonrentals	
EA 11010	LK53 FDB	11/03	WJ	WJ	11/10	Dawsonrentals	
EA 11011	LK53 FBE	10/03	WJ	WJ	11/10	Dawsonrentals	
EA 11012	LK53 FBF	11/03	WJ	WJ	11/10	Dawsonrentals	
EA 11013	LK53 FBG	11/03	WJ	WJ	11/10	Dawsonrentals	
EA 11014	LK53 FBJ	10/03	WJ	WJ	11/10	Dawsonrentals	
EA 11015	LK53 FBL	11/03	WJ	WJ	11/10	Dawsonrentals	
EA 11016	LK53 FBN	10/03	WJ	WJ	11/10	Dawsonrentals	
EA 11017	LK53 FBO	11/03	WJ	WJ	11/10	Dawsonrentals	
EA 11018	LK53 FBU	10/03	WJ	WJ	11/10	Dawsonrentals	
EA 11019	LK53 FBV	10/03	WJ	WJ	11/10	Dawsonrentals	
EA 11020	LK53 FBX	11/03	WJ	WJ	11/10	Dawsonrentals	
EA 11021	LK53 FBY	11/03	WJ	WJ	11/10	Dawsonrentals	
EA 11022	LK53 FBZ	11/03	WJ	WJ	11/10	Dawsonrentals	
EA 11023	LK53 FCA	11/03	WJ	WJ	11/10	Dawsonrentals	

EA 11024	LK53 FCC	11/03	WJ	WJ	11/10	Dawsonrentals	
EA 11025	LK53 FCD	11/03	WJ	WJ	11/10	Dawsonrentals	
EA 11026	LK53 FCE	11/03	WJ	WJ	11/10	Dawsonrentals	
EA 11027	LK53 FCM	11/03	WJ	WJ	11/10	Dawsonrentals	
EA 11028	LK53 FCN	11/03	WJ	WJ	11/10	Dawsonrentals	
EA 11029	LK53 FCO	11/03	WJ	WJ	11/10	Dawsonrentals	
EA 11030	LK53 FCP	11/03	WJ	WJ	11/10	Dawsonrentals	
EA 11031	LK53 FCU	11/03	WJ	WJ	11/10	Dawsonrentals	
EA 11032	LK53 FCV	11/03	WJ	HS	11/10	Dawsonrentals	
EA 11039	LK54 FKW	02/05	HS	HS	12/11	Lombard Finance	
EA 11040	LK54 FKX	02/05	HS	HS	12/11	Lombard Finance	
EA 11041	LK05 FDC	03/05	HS	HS	12/11	Lombard Finance	
EA 11042	LK05 FDD	03/05	HS	HS	12/11	Lombard Finance	
EA 11043	LK05 FDE	03/05	HS	HS	12/11	Lombard Finance	
EA 11044	LK05 FDF	03/05	HS	HS	12/11	Lombard Finance	
EA 11045	LK05 FDJ	03/05	HS	HS	12/11	Lombard Finance	
EA 11046	LK05 FDG	03/05	HS	HS	12/11	Lombard Finance	
EA 11047	LK05 FDL	03/05	HS	HS	12/11	Lombard Finance	
EA 11048	LK05 EZW	03/05	HS	HS	12/11	Lombard Finance	
EA 11049	LK05 EZX	03/05	HS	HS	12/11	Lombard Finance	
EA 11050	LK05 EZZ	03/05	HS	HS	12/11	Lombard Finance	
EA 11051	LK05 FCM	03/05	HS	HS	12/11	Lombard Finance	
EA 11052	LK05 FCN	03/05	HS	HS	12/11	Lombard Finance	
EA 11053	LK05 FCO	03/05	HS	HS	12/11	Lombard Finance	
EA 11054	LK05 FCP	03/05	HS	HS	12/11	Lombard Finance	
EA 11055	LK05 FCU	03/05	HS	HS	12/11	Lombard Finance	
EA 11056	LK05 FCV	03/05	HS	HS	12/11	Lombard Finance	
EA 11057	LK05 FBY	03/05	HS	HS	12/11	Lombard Finance	
EA 11058	LK05 FCX	03/05	HS	HS	12/11	Lombard Finance	
EA 11059	LK05 FCY	03/05	HS	HS	12/11	Lombard Finance	
EA 11060	LK05 FCZ	03/05	HS	HS	12/11	Lombard Finance	
EA 11061	LK05 FDA	03/05	HS	HS	12/11	Lombard Finance	
EA 11062	LK05 FBZ	03/05	HS	HS	12/11	Lombard Finance	
EA 11063	LK05 FCA	03/05	HS	HS	12/11	Lombard Finance	
EA 11064	LK05 FCD	03/05	HS	HS	12/11	Lombard Finance	
EA 11065	LK05 FCC	03/05	HS	HS	12/11	Lombard Finance	
EA 11066	LV52 VFW	12/02	WJ	WJ	11/10	Dawsonrentals	S
EA 11067	LV52 VFX	02/03	WJ	WJ	11/10	Dawsonrentals	S
EA 11068	LV52 VFY	02/03	WJ	WJ	11/10	Dawsonrentals	S
EA 11069	LV52 VFZ	02/03	WJ	WJ	11/10	Dawsonrentals	S
EA 11084	LX03 HDH	03/03	HS	HS		Store	S

Notes to First London Fleet List

Many of the early members of the first batch of these vehicles (2003) were originally numbered in the local ECA 30xx series, starting at ECA 3001, before being renumbered into First's national numbering scheme (110xx) in November 2003.

EA11001-32/66-9 were withdrawn following conversion of route 18 to double-deck operation

Depot Codes: WJ = Willesden Junction   HS = Hayes

Key to notes column D= ex Evobus demonstrator   S=ex Selkent vehicles 23001-4/24 resp. acquired 9/06 (11066-9) or 11/08 (11084) via Dawsonrentals

Table 4   London Central/London General {Go Ahead}

Fleet No.	Reg. No.	New	1st alloc.	Final alloc.	Withdrawn	Initial disposal	Notes
MAL 1	BX02 YZE	05/02	RA	Q	11/11	Store	R,G,C
MAL 2	BX02 YZG	05/02	RA	RA	08/09	CT Plus, Bristol MCA 13	R,G
MAL 3	BX02 YZH	05/02	RA	RA	08/09	Brighton & Hove 101	R,G
MAL 4	BX02 YZJ	05/02	RA	RA	08/09	Lombard Finance	R,G
MAL 5	BX02 YZK	05/02	RA	Q	08/09	CT Plus, Bristol MCA 14	R,G,C
MAL 6	BX02 YZL	05/02	RA	RA	08/09	Lombard Finance	R,G
MAL 7	BX02 YZM	05/02	RA	RA	08/09	Brighton & Hove 102	R,G
MAL 8	BX02 YZN	05/02	RA	RA	08/09	Lombard Finance	R,G
MAL 9	BX02 YZO	05/02	RA	RA	08/09	CT Plus, Bristol MCA 16	R,G,C
MAL 10	BX02 YZP	05/02	RA	NX	08/09	Brighton & Hove 103	R,G
MAL 11	BX02 YYS	05/02	RA	RA	08/09	CT Plus, Bristol MCA 23	R,G,C
MAL 12	BX02 YYT	05/02	RA	Q	11/11	Store	R,G
MAL 13	BX02 YYU	05/02	RA	RA	08/09	CT Plus, Bristol MCA 22	R,G
MAL 14	BX02 YYV	05/02	RA	RA	08/09	CT Plus, Bristol MCA 19	R,G
MAL 15	BX02 YYZ	05/02	RA	RA	08/09	Wilts & Dorset 4001	R,G
MAL 16	BX02 YYW	05/02	RA	RA	08/09	Brighton & Hove 104	R,G
MAL 17	BX02 YZA	05/02	RA	RA	08/09	Lombard Finance	R,G
MAL 18	BX02 YZB	05/02	RA	RA	08/09	Lombard Finance	R,G
MAL 19	BX02 YZC	05/02	RA	RA	08/09	Bus Business, Witney	R,G
MAL 20	BX02 YZD	05/02	RA	Q	08/09	Lombard Finance	R,G,C
MAL 21	BX02 YYJ	05/02	RA	RA	08/09	CT Plus, Bristol MCA 24	R,G
MAL 22	BX02 YYK	05/02	RA	RA	08/09	Lombard Finance	R,G
MAL 23	BX02 YYL	05/02	RA	RA	08/09	Lombard Finance	R,G
MAL 24	BX02 YYM	05/02	RA	RA	08/09	CT Plus, Bristol MCA 21	R,G,C
MAL 25	BX02 YYN	05/02	RA	NX	08/09	Store	R,G
MAL 26	BX02 YYO	05/02	RA	RA	08/09	Lombard Finance	R,G
MAL 27	BX02 YYP	05/02	RA	RA	08/09	CT Plus, Bristol MCA 20	R,G,C
MAL 28	BX02 YYR	05/02	RA	Q	08/09	Lombard Finance	R,G
MAL 29	BX02 YZR	05/02	RA	RA	08/09	CT Plus, Bristol MCA 17	R,G
MAL 30	BX02 YZS	05/02	RA	Q	08/09	CT Plus, Bristol MCA 15	R,G
MAL 31	BX02 YZT	05/02	RA	RA	08/09	CT Plus, Bristol MCA 18	R,G

MAL 32	BN52 GWC	NX	NX	01/03	11/11	Store	C
MAL33	BN52 GWD	NX	NX	01/03	11/11	Store	C
MAL 34	BN52 GWE	NX	NX	12/02	11/11	Store	C
MAL 35	BN52 GVU	NX	NX	01/03	11/11	Store	C
MAL 36	BD52 LNN	NX	NX	12/02	12/03	Destroyed by fire Edgeware Road 3 December 2003 on service 436	C
MAL 36	BX04 NBD	NX	NX	05/04	11/11	Store	C, RP
MAL 37	BD52 LNO	NX	NX	01/03	11/11	Store	C
MAL 38	BD52 LNP	NX	NX	12/02	11/11	Store	C
MAL 39	BD52 LNR	NX	NX	12/02	11/11	Store	C
MAL 40	BD52 LNT	NX	NX	01/03	11/11	Store	C
MAL 41	BD52 LNU	NX	NX	01/03	11/11	Store	C
MAL 42	BD52 LMU	NX	NX	01/03	11/11	Store	C
MAL 43	BD52 LMV	NX	NX	01/03	11/11	Store	C
MAL 44	BD52 LMX	NX	NX	01/03	11/11	Store	C
MAL 45	BD52 LMY	NX	NX	01/03	11/11	Store	C
MAL 46	BD52 LNA	NX	NX	01/03	11/11	Store	C
MAL 47	BD52 LNC	NX	NX	01/03	11/11	Store	C
MAL 48	BD52 LNE	NX	NX	01/03	11/11	Store	C
MAL 49	BD52 LNF	NX	NX	01/03	11/11	Store	C
MAL 50	BD52 LNG	NX	NX	01/03	11/11	Store	C
MAL 51	BD52 LNH	NX	NX	01/03	02/04	Destroyed by fire Camberwell New Rd 7 February 2004 on service 436	C
MAL 51	BU04 EZK	NX	NX	06/04	11/11	Store	C, RP
MAL 52	BD52 LMO	NX	NX	01/03	11/11	Store	C
MAL 53	BL52 ODK	NX	NX	01/03	11/11	Store	C
MAL 54	BL52 ODM	NX	NX	01/03	11/11	Store	C
MAL 55	BL52 ODN	NX	NX	01/03	11/11	Store	C
MAL 56	BL52 ODP	NX	NX	01/03	11/11	Store	C
MAL 57	BL52 ODR	NX	NX	01/03	11/11	Store	C
MAL 58	BL52 ODS	NX	NX	01/03	03/04	Destroyed by fire in Park Lane 9 April 2004 on service 436	C
MAL 58	BU04 UTM	NX	NX	07/04	11/11	Store	C, RP
MAL 59	BL52 ODT	NX	NX	01/03	11/11	Store	C
MAL 60	BL52 ODU	NX	NX	01/03	11/11	Store	C
MAL 61	BL52 ODV	NX	NX	01/03	11/11	Store	C
MAL 62	BX54 EFC	Q	Q	11/04	11/11	Brighton & Hove 115	C
MAL 63	BX54 EFD	Q	Q	11/04	11/11	Brighton & Hove 116	C
MAL 64	BX54 UCM	Q	Q	11/04	11/11	Brighton & Hove 117	C
MAL 65	BX54 UCN	Q	Q	11/04	11/11	Brighton & Hove 118	C
MAL 66	BX54 UCO	Q	Q	11/04		London Central commercial fleet	C
MAL 67	BX54 UCP	Q	Q	11/04	11/11	Go Ahead North East 5349	C
MAL 68	BX54 UCR	Q	Q	11/04	11/11	Go Ahead North East 5350	C
MAL 69	BX54 UCT	Q	Q	11/04		London Central commercial fleet	C

MAL 70	BX54 UCU		11/04	Q	11/11	Go Ahead North East 5351	C
MAL 71	BX54 UCV		11/04	Q	11/11	Go Ahead North East 5352	C
MAL 72	BX54 UCW		11/04	Q	11/11	Go Ahead North East 5353	C
MAL 73	BX54 UCZ		11/04	Q	11/11	Go Ahead North East 5354	C
MAL 74	BX54 UDB		11/04	Q	11/11	Go Ahead North East 5355	C
MAL 75	BX54 UDD		11/04	Q	11/11	Go AheadNorth East 5356	C
MAL 76	BX54 UDE		11/04	Q	11/11	Go South Coast events fleet (I.O.W)	C
MAL 77	BX54 UDG		11/04	Q	11/11	Go South Coast events fleet (I.O.W)	C
MAL 78	BX54 UDH		09/04	Q	11/11	London Central commercial fleet	C
MAL 79	BX54 UDJ		11/04	Q	11/11	London Central commercial fleet	C
MAL 80	BX54 UDK		11/04	Q	11/11	Konectbus 805	C
MAL 81	BX54 UDL		11/04	Q	11/11	Go South Coast events fleet (I.O.W)	C
MAL 82	BX54 UDM		09/04	Q	11/11	London Central commercial fleet	C
MAL 83	BX54 UDN		11/04	Q	11/11	Go South Coast events fleet (I.O.W)	C
MAL 84	BX54 UDO		10/04	Q	11/11	Go South Coast events fleet (I.O.W)	C
MAL 85	BX54 UDP		10/04	Q	11/11	London Central commercial fleet	C
MAL 86	BX54 UDT		11/04	Q	11/11	Go South Coast events fleet (I.O.W)	C
MAL 87	BX54 UDU		11/04	Q	11/11	Go South Coast events fleet (I.O.W)	C
MAL 88	BX54 UDV		10/04	Q	11/11	Konectbus 806	C
MAL 89	BX54 UDW		11/04	Q	11/11	Go South Coast events fleet (I.O.W)	C
MAL 90	BX54 UDY		11/04	Q	11/11	Go South Coast events fleet	C
MAL 91	BX54 UDZ		11/04	Q	11/11	Go South Coast events fleet (I.O.W)	C
MAL 92	BX54 UEA		11/04	Q	11/11	Konectbus 807	C
MAL 93	BX54 UEB		11/04	Q	11/11	Go South Coast events fleet	C
MAL 94	BX54 EFB		11/04	Q	11/11	Go South Coast events fleet	C
MAL 95	BD57 WCY		02/08	MW	09/11	Konectbus 801	G
MAL 96	BD57 WCZ		02/08	MW	09/11	Konectbus 802	G
MAL 97	BD57 WDA		02/08	MW	09/11	Konectbus 800	G
MAL 98	BD57 WDC		02/08	MW	09/11	Brighton & Hove 105	G
MAL 99	BD57 WDE		02/08	MW	09/11	Brighton & Hove 106	G
MAL 100	BD57 WDK		02/08	MW	09/11	Brighton & Hove 107	G
MAL 101	BD57 WDL		02/08	MW	09/11	Brighton & Hove 108	G
MAL 102	BD57 WDM		02/08	MW	09/11	Brighton & Hove 109	G
MAL 103	BD57 WDN		02/08	MW	09/11	Brighton & Hove 110	G
MAL 104	BD57 WDP		01/08	MW	09/11	Brighton & Hove 111	G
MAL 105	BD57 WDR		02/08	MW	09/11	Brighton & Hove 112	G
MAL 106	BD57 WDS		02/08	MW	09/11	Brighton & Hove 113	G
MAL 107	BD57 WDT		02/08	MW	09/11	Brighton & Hove 114	G
MAL 108	BL 57 OXJ		02/08	MW	09/11	Go-Ahead North East 5339	G
MAL 109	BL57 OXK		02/08	MW	09/11	Go-Ahead North East 5340	G
MAL 110	BL57 OXM		02/08	MW	11/11	Konectbus 803	G, C
MAL 111	BL57 OXN		02/08	Q	11/11	Konectbus 804	G, C
MAL 112	BL57 OXP		02/08	MW	09/11	Go-Ahead North East 5341	G
MAL 113	BP57 UYE		02/08	MW	09/11	Go-Ahead North East 5342	G

MAL 114	BP57 UYF	02/08	MW	MW	09/11	Go-Ahead North East 5343	G
MAL 115	BP57 UYG	02/08	MW	MW	09/11	Go-Ahead North East 5344	G
MAL 116	BP57 UYH	02/08	MW	MW	09/11	Go-Ahead North East 5345	G
MAL 117	BP57 UYJ	02/08	MW	MW	09/11	Go-Ahead North East 5346	G
MAL 118	BP57 UYK	02/08	MW	MW	09/11	Go-Ahead North East 5347	G
MAL 119	BP57 UYL	02/08	MW	MW	09/11	Go-Ahead North East 5348	G
MAL 120	LX03 HDV	03/03	Q	Q	00/11	Unknown, possibly Dawsonrentals	C, S

Notes to London Central/General Fleet List

Depot Codes: MW = Mandela Way, Southwark   NX = New Cross   Q = Camberwell   RA = Waterloo

Key to Notes Column   C=London Central   G= London General   R=Red Arrow branding   RP= Replacement bus bearing same fleet number   S= Ex Selkent 23030 09/08 via Dawsonrentals

MAL 95-119 had 47 seats

MAL 1-31 withdrawn following conversion of Routes 507/521 to Citaro saloons August 2009.

Table 5   Arriva London North

Fleet No.	Reg. No.	New	1st alloc.	Final alloc.	Withdrawn	Initial disposal	Notes
MA 1	BX04 MWW	04/04	EC	EC	11/09	store	
MA 2	BX04 MWY	03/04	EC	EC	09/11	store	
MA 3	BX04 MWZ	04/04	EC	LV	09/11	store	
MA 4	BX04 MXA	03/04	EC	EC	09/11	store	
MA 5	BX04 MXB 205 CLT 10/05	03/04	EC	EC	11/09	Arriva Merseyside 6005 (via Arriva North West)	R1
MA 6	BX04 MXC	03/04	EC	EC	11/09	Arriva Merseyside 6006 (via Arriva North West)	
MA 7	BX04 MXD	03/04	EC	EC	11/11	store	
MA 8	BX04 MXE	03/04	EC	LV	09/11	store	
MA 9	BX04 MXG	03/04	EC	EC	11/09	Arriva Merseyside 6009 then Arriva Midlands 5002	
MA 10	BX04 MXH	03/04	EC	EC	11/09	Arriva Midlands 5004	
MA 11	BX04 MXJ	03/04	EC	EC	11/11	store	
MA 12	BX04 MXK	03/04	EC	EC	11/09	Arriva Merseyside 6012 then Arriva Midlands 5001	
MA 13	BX04 MXL	03/04	EC	EC	11/09	Arriva North West	
MA 14	BX04 MXM	03/04	EC	EC	11/09	Arriva Merseyside 6014 (via Arriva North West)	
MA 15	BX04 MXN	03/04	EC	EC	11/11	store	
MA 16	BX04 MXP	03/04	EC	EC	11/11	store	
MA 17	BX04 MXR 217 CLT 12/05	03/04	EC	EC	11/09	National Express, Stansted	R2
MA 18	BX04 MXS	03/04	EC	EC	11/11	store	
MA 19	BX04 MXT 519 CLT 12/05	04/04	EC	EC	11/09	Arriva North West	R3

MA 20	BX04 MXU	EC	EC	04/04	09/11	store	
MA 21	BX04 MXV	EC	EC	04/04	11/09	Arriva North West	
MA 22	BX04 MXW	EC	EC	03/04	11/11	store	
MA 23	BX04 MXY	EC	EC	03/04	11/09	Arriva North West	
MA 24	BX04 MXZ 324 CLT 01/06	EC	EC	04/04	11/09	Arriva North West	R4
MA 25	BX04 MYA	EC	EC	03/04	11/09	Arriva Midlands 5003	
MA 26	BX04 MYB	EC	EC	03/04	11/11	store	
MA 27	BX04 MYC	EC	EC	04/04	11/11	store	
MA 28	BX04 MYD	EC	LV	03/04	09/11	store	
MA 29	BX04 MYF	EC	EC	04/04	11/11	store	
MA 30	BX04 MYY 330 CLT 12/05	LV	LV	05/04	09/11	store	R5
MA 31	BX04 MZF	LV	EC	06/04	11/11	store	
MA 32	BX04 NDD	LV	LV	05/04	11/09	Arriva North West	
MA 33	BX04 NDG	LV	LV	05/04	11/09	Arriva Merseyside 6033 (via Arriva North West)	
MA 34	BX04 NDU	LV	EC	06/04	11/11	store	
MA 35	BX04 NDV	LV	EC	05/04	09/11	store	
MA 36	BX04 NDY	LV	LV	06/04	09/11	store	
MA 37	BX04 NDZ	LV	EC	06/04	11/11	store	
MA 38	BX04 NEF	LV	EC	06/04	11/11	store	
MA 39	BX04 NEJ	LV	EC	06/04	11/11	store	
MA 40	BX04 MYG	LV	LV	10/04	11/09	Arriva Merseyside 6040 then Arriva Midlands 5000	
MA 41	BX04 MYH	LV	LV	07/04	11/09	Arriva North West	
MA 42	BX04 MYJ	LV	LV	07/04	09/11	Arriva Malta	
MA 43	BX04 MYK	LV	EC	08/04	11/11	store	
MA 44	BX04 MYL	LV	EC	08/04	11/11	store	
MA 45	BX04 MYM	LV	EC	08/04	11/11	store	
MA 46	BX04 NYN	LV	LV	08/04	09/11	Arriva Malta	
MA 47	BX04 NYR	LV	LV	08/04	09/11	Arriva Malta	
MA 48	BX04 MYS	LV	EC	08/04	11/11	Arriva Malta	
MA 49	BX04 MYT	LV	EC	08/04	11/11	store	
MA 50	BX04 MYU	LV	LV	07/04	09/11	Arriva Malta	
MA 51	BX04 MYV	LV	LV	07/04	09/11	Arriva Malta	
MA 52	BX04 MYW	LV	LV	07/04	09/11	Arriva Malta	
MA 53	BX04 MYZ	LV	LV	07/04	09/11	Arriva Malta	
MA54	BX04 MZD	LV	LV	07/04	01/11	Fire Victim (Del 06/10)	
MA 55	BX04 MZE	LV	LV	07/04	09/11	store	
MA 56	BX04 MZG	LV	LV	07/04	09/11	store	
MA 57	BX04 MZJ	LV	LV	08/04	09/11	store	
MA 58	BX04 MZL	LV	LV	08/04	09/11	store	
MA 59	BX04 MZN	LV	EC	07/04	11/11	store	
MA 60	BX04 NBK	LV	LV	07/04	09/11	store	

No.	Registration	Date	Op1	Op2	Date2	Disposal	Notes
MA 61	BX04 NBL 361 CLT 12/05	07/04	LV	LV	09/11	Arriva Malta	R6
MA 62	BX04 NCF	07/04	LV	LV	09/11	store	
MA 63	BX04 NCJ	07/04	LV	EC	11/11	store	
MA 64	BX04 NCN	07/04	LV	EC	11/11	store	
MA 65	BX04 NCU	07/04	LV	EC	11/11	store	
MA 66	BX04 NCV	07/04	LV	EC	11/11	store	
MA 67	BX04 NCY	07/04	LV	LV	09/11	store	
MA 68	BX04 NCZ	07/04	LV	LV	09/11	Arriva Malta	
MA 69	BX04 NDC	07/04	LV	LV	09/11	Arriva Malta	
MA 70	BX04 NDE 70 CLT 12/05	08/04	LV	LV	09/11	store	R7
MA 71	BX04 NDF	08/04	LV	EC	11/11	store	
MA 72	BX04 NDJ	07/04	LV	LV	09/11	store	
MA 73	BX04 NDK	08/04	LV	LV	09/11	store	
MA 74	BX04 NDL	08/04	LV	LV	09/11	store	
MA 75	BX04 NDN	08/04	LV	EC	11/11	store	
MA 76	BX04 NEN	08/04	LV	LV	09/11	Arriva Malta	
MA 77	BX05 UWV	07/05	AE	LV	09/11	store	
MA 78	BX05 UWW	08/05	AE	EC	11/11	store	
MA 79`	BX05 UWY	07/05	AE	LV	09/11	store	
MA 80	BX05 UWZ 480 CLT 12/05	07/05	AE	EC	11/11	Arriva Malta	R8
MA 81	BU05 VFE	08/05	AE	EC	11/11	store	
MA 82	BU05 VFF	08/05	AE	LV	06/11	Fire victim	
MA 83	BX05 UXC	08/05	AE	EC	11/11	store	
MA 84	BU 05 VFG	08/05	AE	EC	11/11	store	
MA 85	BU05 VFD 185 CLT 10/05	07/05	AE	EC	11/11	Arriva Malta	R9
MA 86	BU05 VFH	08/05	AE	EC	11/11	store	
MA 87	BU05 VFJ	08/05	AE	EC	11/11	store	
MA 88	BX05 UXD	07/05	AE	LV	09/11	store	
MA 89	BX55 FWA	09/05	AE	LV	09/11	store	
MA 90	BX55 FWB	09/05	AE	LV	09/11	Arriva Malta	
MA 91	BX55 FUH	09/05	AE	EC	11/11	store	
MA 92	BX55 FUJ	09/05	AE	EC	11/11	store	
MA 93	BX55 FUM 593 CLT 12/05	09/05	AE	LV	09/11	Arriva Malta	R10
MA 94	BX55 FUO	09/05	AE	EC	11/11	store	
MA 95	BX55 FUP	09/05	AE	EC	11/11	store	
MA 96	BX55 FUT	09/05	AE	EC	09/11	store	
MA 97	BX55 FUU	09/05	AE	EC	11/11	store	
MA 98	BX55 FUV 398 CLT 12/05	09/05	AE	EC	11/11	store	R11, A
MA 99	BX55 FUW	09/05	AE	EC	11/11	store	

Fleet No.	Registration	Date			Date	Operator / Notes	
MA 100	BX55 FUY	09/05	AE	LV	01/11	Arriva Malta BUS 214	
MA 101	BX55 FVA	09/05	AE	LV	01/11	Arriva Malta TR 303 spares	
MA 102	BX55 FVB	09/05	AE	LV	01/11	Arriva Malta BUS 216	
MA 103	BX55 FVC	09/05	AE	LV	01/11	Arriva Malta BUS 220	
MA 104	BX55 FVD	09/05	AE	LV	01/11	Arriva Malta BUS 204	
MA 105	BX55 FVF	09/05	AE	LV	01/11	Arriva Malta BUS 203	
MA 106	BX55 FVG	09/05	AE	LV	01/11	Arriva Malta BUS 224	
MA 107	BX55 FVH	09/05	AE	LV	01/11	Arriva Malta BUS 225	
MA 108	BX55 FVJ	09/05	AE	LV	01/11	Arriva Malta BUS 226	
MA 109	BX55 FVK	09/05	AE	LV	01/11	Arriva Malta BUS 227	
MA 110	BX55 FVL	09/05	AE	LV	01/11	Arriva Malta BUS 205	
MA 111	BX55 FVM	09/05	AE	LV	01/11	Arriva Malta BUS 228	
MA 112	BX55 FVN	09/05	AE	LV	01/11	Arriva Malta BUS 229	
MA 113	BX55 FVO	09/05	AE	LV	01/11	Arriva, Malta BUS 206	
MA 114	BX55 FVP	09/05	AE	LV	01/11	Arriva, Malta BUS 222	
MA 115	BX55 FVR	09/05	AE	LV	01/11	Arriva, Malta BUS 215	
MA 116	BX55 FVS	09/05	AE	LV	01/11	Arriva, Malta BUS 230	
MA 117	BX55 FVT	09/05	AE	LV	01/11	Arriva, Malta BUS 231	
MA 118	BX55 FVU	09/05	AE	LV	01/11	Arriva, Malta BUS 207	
MA 119	BX55 FVV / 319 CLT 12/05	09/05	AE	LV	01/11	Arriva, Malta BUS 208	R12
MA 120	BX55 FVW	09/05	AE	LV	01/11	Arriva, Malta BUS 219	
MA 121	BX55 FVY	09/05	AE	LV	01/11	Arriva, Malta BUS 209	
MA 122	BX55 FVZ	09/05	AE	LV	09/10	Fire victim	
MA 123	BX55 FWG	09/05	AE	LV	01/11	Arriva, Malta TR 302	
MA 124	BX55 FWH / 124 CLT 12/05	09/05	AE	EC	03/11	Arriva, Malta BUS 232	R13
MA 125	BX55 FWJ	10/05	EC	EC	01/11	Arriva, Malta BUS 218	
MA 126	BX55 FWK	10/05	EC	EC	01/11	Arriva, Malta BUS 233	
MA 127	BX55 FWL	10/05	EC	EC	01/11	Arriva, Malta BUS 234	
MA 128	BX55 FWM	10/05	EC	EC	01/11	Arriva, Malta BUS 235	
MA 129	BX55 FWN	10/05	EC	EC	01/11	Arriva, Malta BUS 236	
MA 130	BX55 FWP	10/05	EC	EC	01/11	Arriva, Malta BUS 210	
MA 131	BX55 FWR	11/05	AE	EC	01/11	Arriva, Malta BUS 237	
MA 132	BX55 FWS	11/05	AE	EC	01/11	Arriva, Malta BUS 238	
MA 133	BX55 FWT	11/05	AE	EC	01/11	Arriva, Malta BUS 239	
MA 134	BX55 FWU	11/05	AE	EC	01/11	Arriva, Malta BUS 211	
MA 135	BX55 FWV	11/05	AE	EC	01/11	Arriva, Malta BUS 240	
MA 136	BX55 FWW	11/05	AE	EC	01/11	Arriva, Malta BUS 241	
MA 137	BX55 FWY	11/05	AE	EC	01/11	Arriva, Malta BUS 242	
MA 138	BX55 FWZ	11/05	AE	EC	01/11	Arriva, Malta BUS 217	
MA 139	BX55 FXB	11/05	AE	EC	01/11	Arriva, Malta BUS 212	
MA 140	BX55 FXC	11/05	AE	EC	01/11	Arriva, Malta BUS 243	
MA 141	BX55 FXE	11/05	EC	EC	01/11	Arriva, Malta BUS 244	